myinspiredlife
COLORING

Mandalas Volume 1: ASIA

Ayesha Hilton

Copyright

First Edition 2015

Copyright © 2015 Ayesha Hilton

All rights reserved. No part of this book may be reproduced or transmitted in any form or by any means, including but not limited to information storage and retrieval systems, electronic, mechanical, photocopy, recording, etc. without written permission from the copyright holder.

National Library of Australia

Cataloguing-in-Publication entry:

Hilton, Ayesha (1973)

My Inspired Life Coloring: Asia Mandalas

1st ed.

ISBN: 978-0-9944229-0-3 (paperback)

Coloring, Creativity, Inspiration

Published by Inspired Life Press
Email: info@InspiredLifePress.com
For further information about orders:
Phone: +61 421 055 408
To see other titles published by Inspired Life Press visit:
www.InspiredLifePress.com

BONUS OFFER

We would love to give you some bonus printable coloring pages for you to enjoy.

We will also keep you up to date with new releases and you will get free coloring pages in your inbox.

When you join, you will also be invited to join our private Facebook group where you can share your works in progress as well as your finished pieces.

Claim Your Bonus Coloring Pages Today

www.MyInspiredLife.Club/asiabonus

Share Your Color

Share your coloring and I will share it with the world!

As a creator of coloring designs, it is so inspiring to see how you apply your individual creativity to the designs.

Connect with me on social media and share your creations!

facebook.com/ayeshahiltonpage   @Ayesha_Hilton   @ayesha_hilton

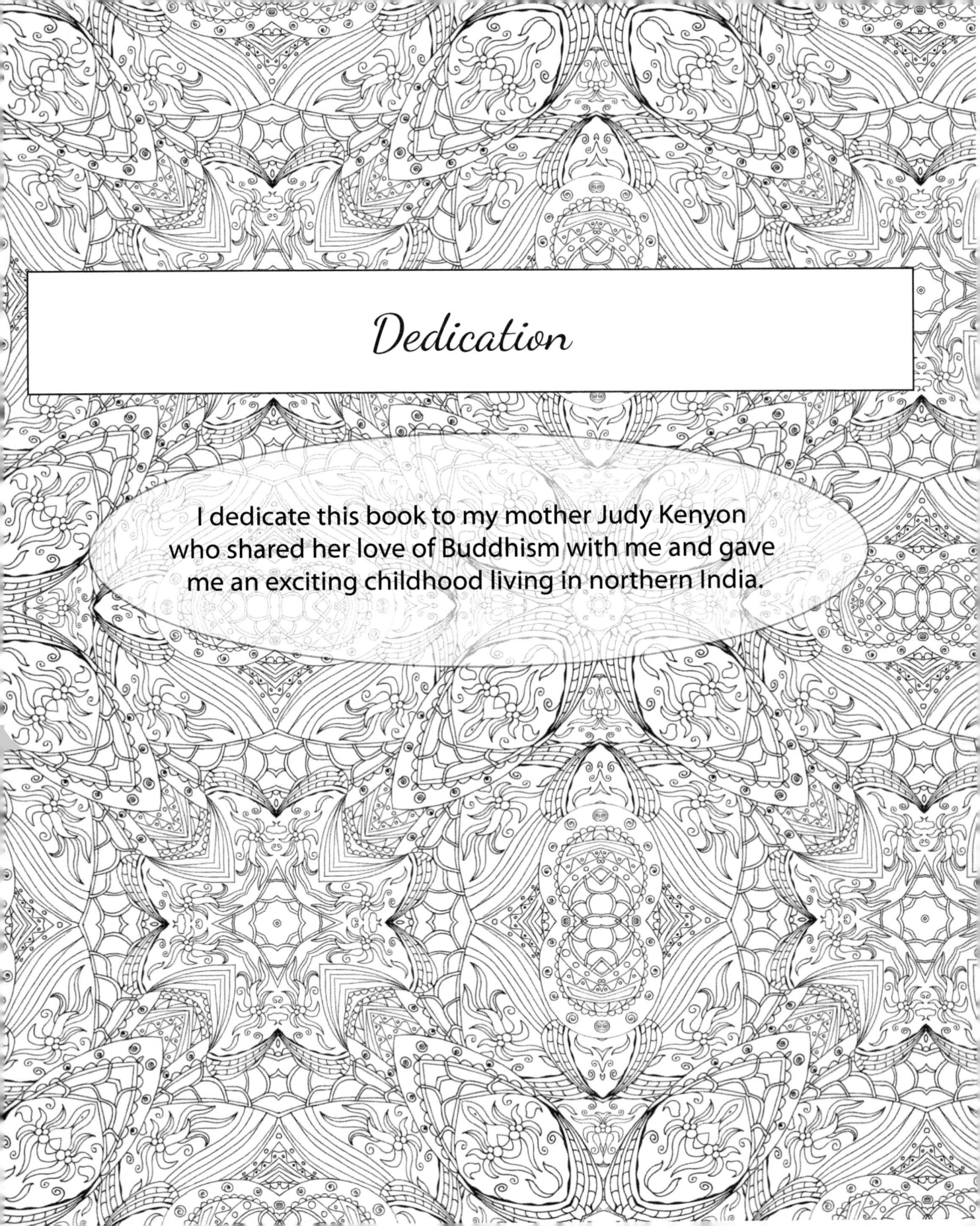

Dedication

I dedicate this book to my mother Judy Kenyon who shared her love of Buddhism with me and gave me an exciting childhood living in northern India.

About Mandalas

Gorgeous Designs Inspired by South East Asia

The designs in this book have been inspired by the cultures and designs of South East Asia. I have lived in India and Thailand, and travelled to Japan, Nepal, Laos and Burma. My mother was one of the first westerners to follow Tibetan Buddhism in the early 1970s. We had the honour and privilege of spending a lot of time with Tibetan Lamas (spiritual teachers) and would see the elaborate mandalas that the monks would create out of colored sand.

It would take days and days of concentration and effort to create elaborate patterns with the sand. At the end, after prayers and blessings, the sand would be swept away. This process showed me the impermanence of life and the beauty that we can enjoy when we let go of attachment to the end result. Each sand mandala would be blessed and prayed over and this is the true essence of the creation of these beautiful mandalas.

The word mandala comes from Sanskrit and loosely translated means circle. A mandala is a symbolic representation of the universe. In psychoanalysis, it represents the dreamer's search for completeness and self-unity. Mandalas are used in many spiritual and meditational practices.

Mandalas appear in all aspects of life, including the celestial circles of the earth, sun and moon, as well as conceptually in our circle of friends, family and community.

I encourage you to enjoy coloring the mandalas in this book without judgement or attachment. Allow yourself to get caught up in the moment and feel the joy that comes from being truly present.

Regardless of your spiritual or religious beliefs, there is no doubt that the simple act of coloring mandalas will bring you greater peace and joy.

Ayesha xox

Benefits of Coloring

Coloring isn't just for kids.

It is is a fun activity for adults that can have enormous benefits.

Here are just some of the reasons coloring is so good for you:

- Creates a sense of wellbeing
- Quietens the mind
- Stimulates the brain
- Provides practice for fine motor skills
- Increases mindfulness and attentiveness
- Allows creativity to flow
- Acts like color therapy for the body and soul
- Anyone can do it - you don't need to be especially creative or artistic

The benefits of coloring have been known by the medical professional for decades. Psychiatrist Carl Jung, the founder of analytical psychology, prescribed coloring to his patients in the early 1900s to calm and center their minds.

It is an activity you can do with your friends, family and colleagues!

Coloring Tips

No Rules
The beauty of coloring is that there are no rules.
Of course, you probably want to color inside the lines,
but other than that you can experiment with different
coloring tools - pens, pencils, crayons, water color pencils, even paints -
and different techniques.

Don't Compare
If you're in any Facebook groups for coloring enthusiasts, you will see
lots of different ways of coloring and some stunning results.
Don't fall into the trap of comparing your coloring to others.
Coloring is for everyone, whether they think of themselves
as creative or artistic or not.
Each person brings their own way of coloring to a piece.

Try New Things
Don't be afraid to experiment and try new ways of coloring.
Try different color combinations,
different mediums, and play around with techniques.

Get Together with Friends & Family
Coloring is an activity you can do easily with friends and family
of all ages and abilities. It's a relaxing activity to do with your children.

Have Fun
Stay calm and color.
This is all about the luscious enjoyment of time spent focused
on doing something that gives you joy.

"You, yourself, as much as anybody in the entire universe, deserve your love and affection."
Buddha

"Do you really want to be happy?

You can begin by being appreciative of who you are and what you've got."

Benjamin Hoff
The Tao of Pooh

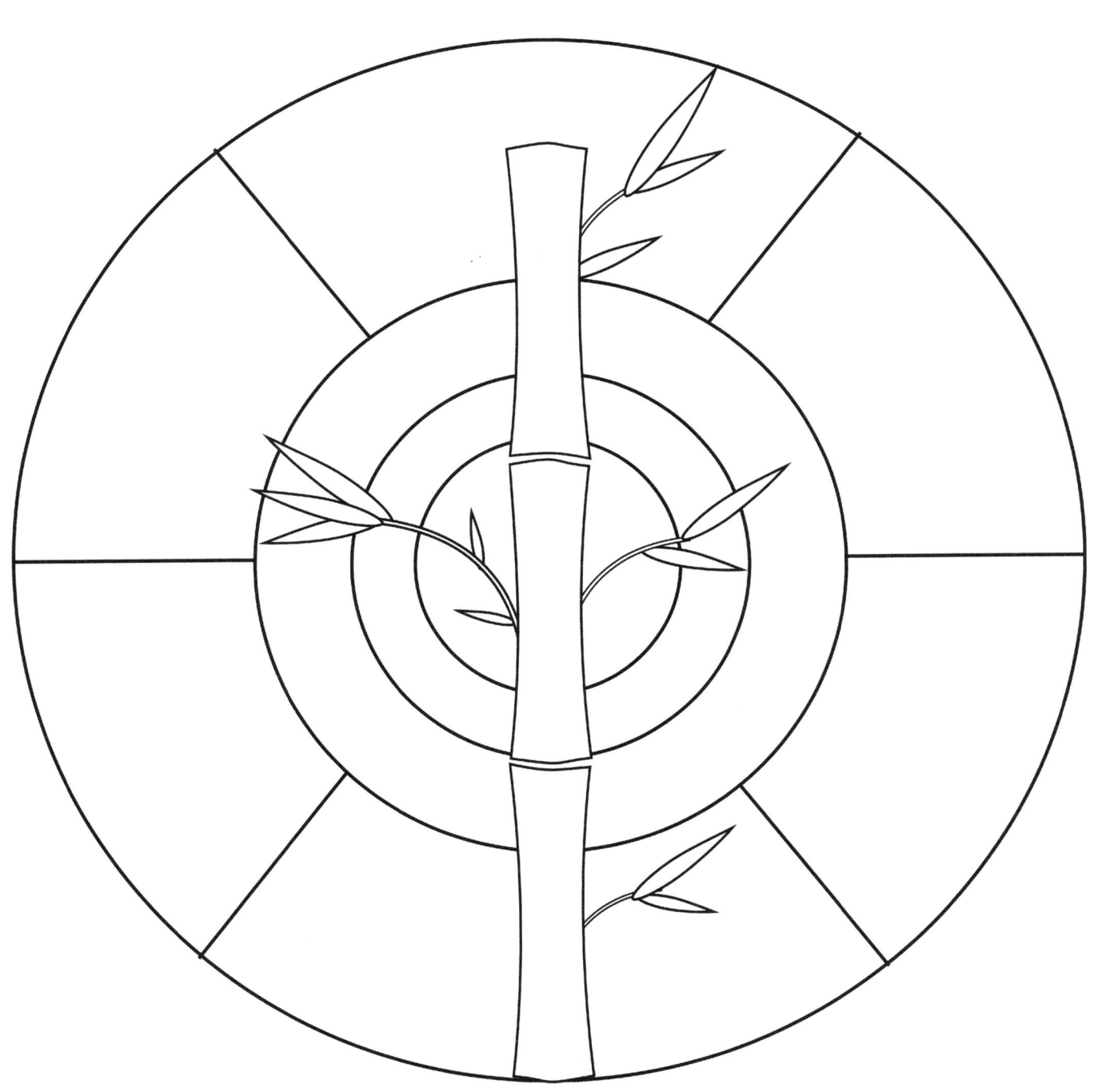

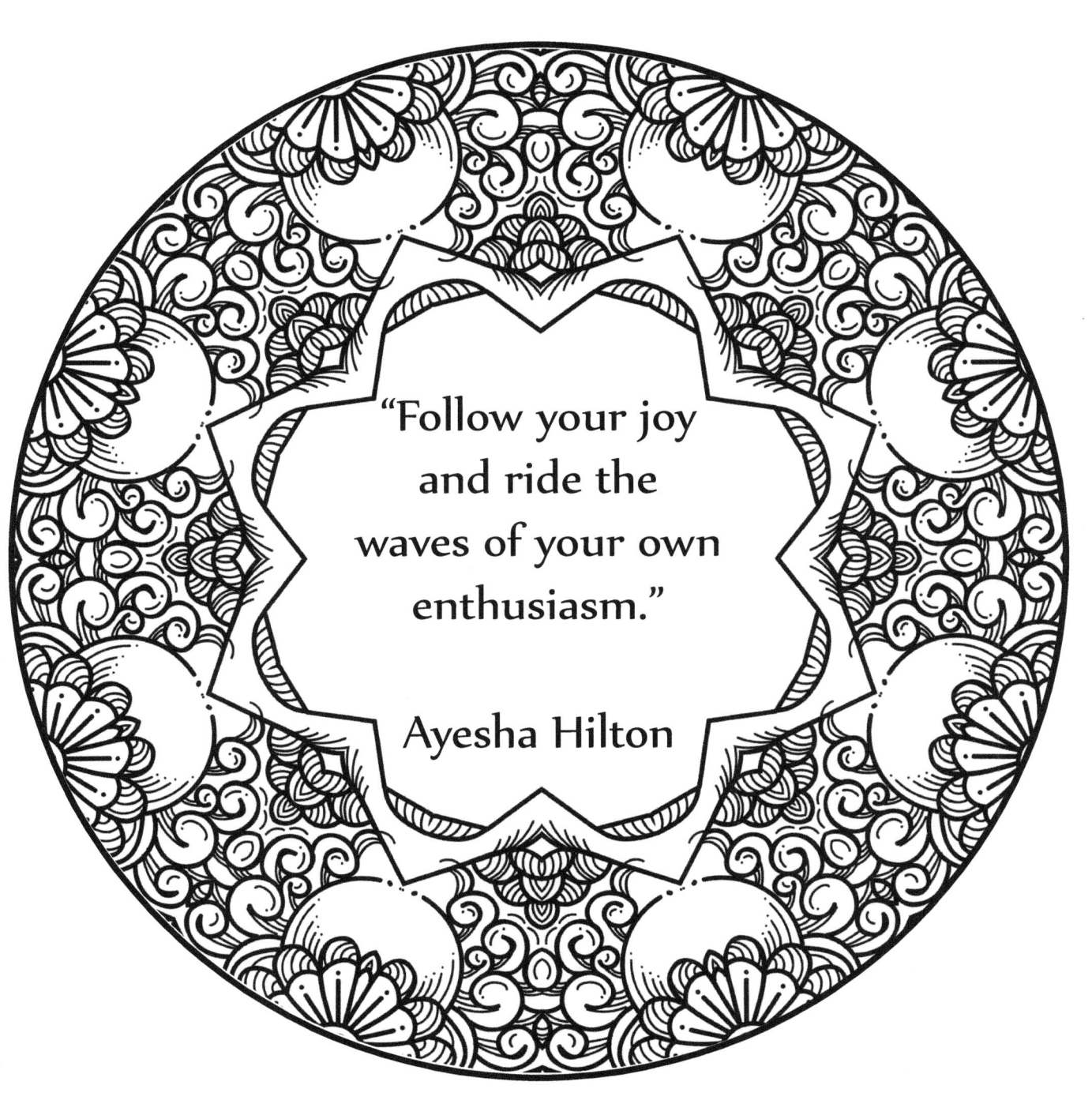

"The clouds above us join and separate,
The breeze in the courtyard leaves and returns,
Life is like that, so why not relax?
Who can stop us from celebrating?"
Lu Yu

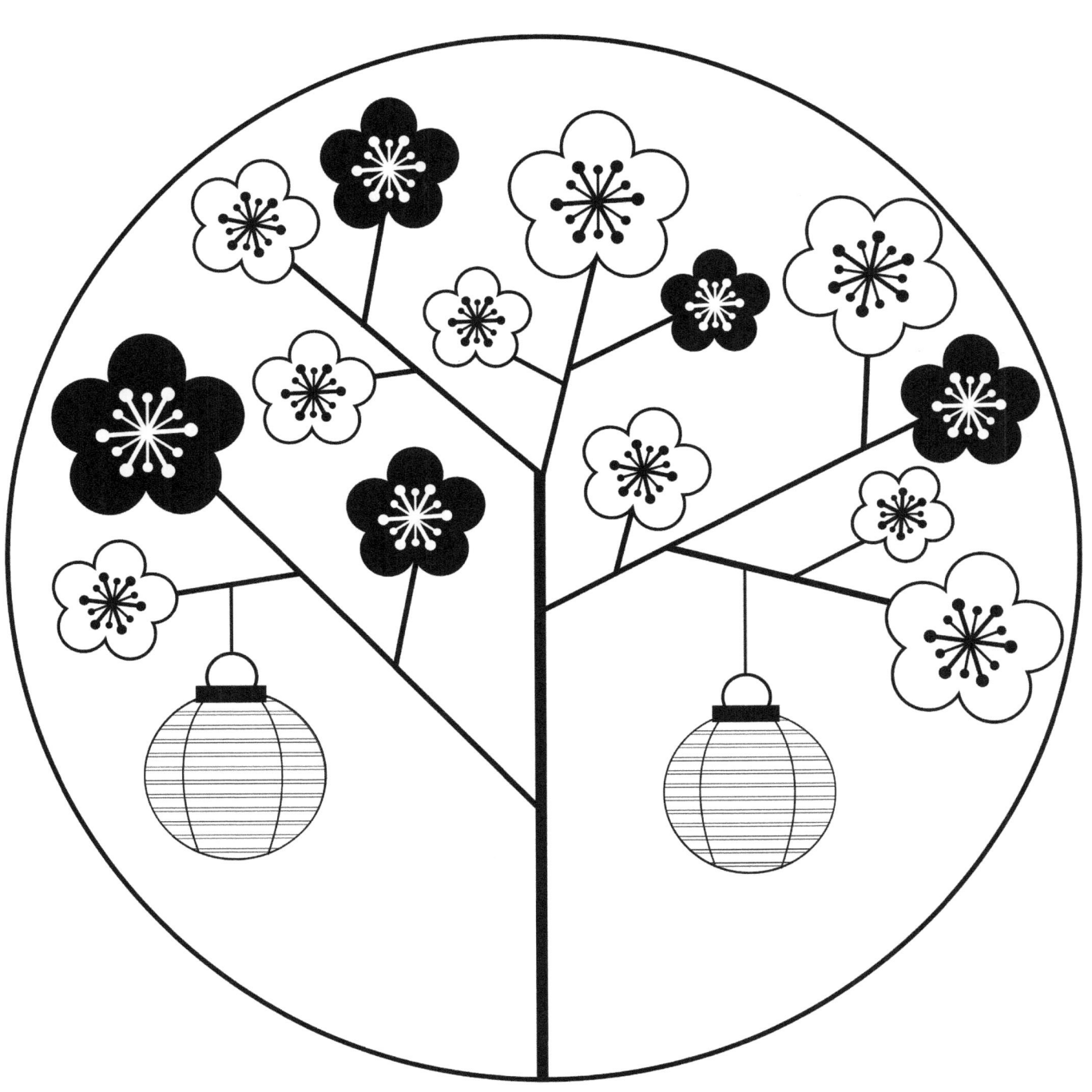

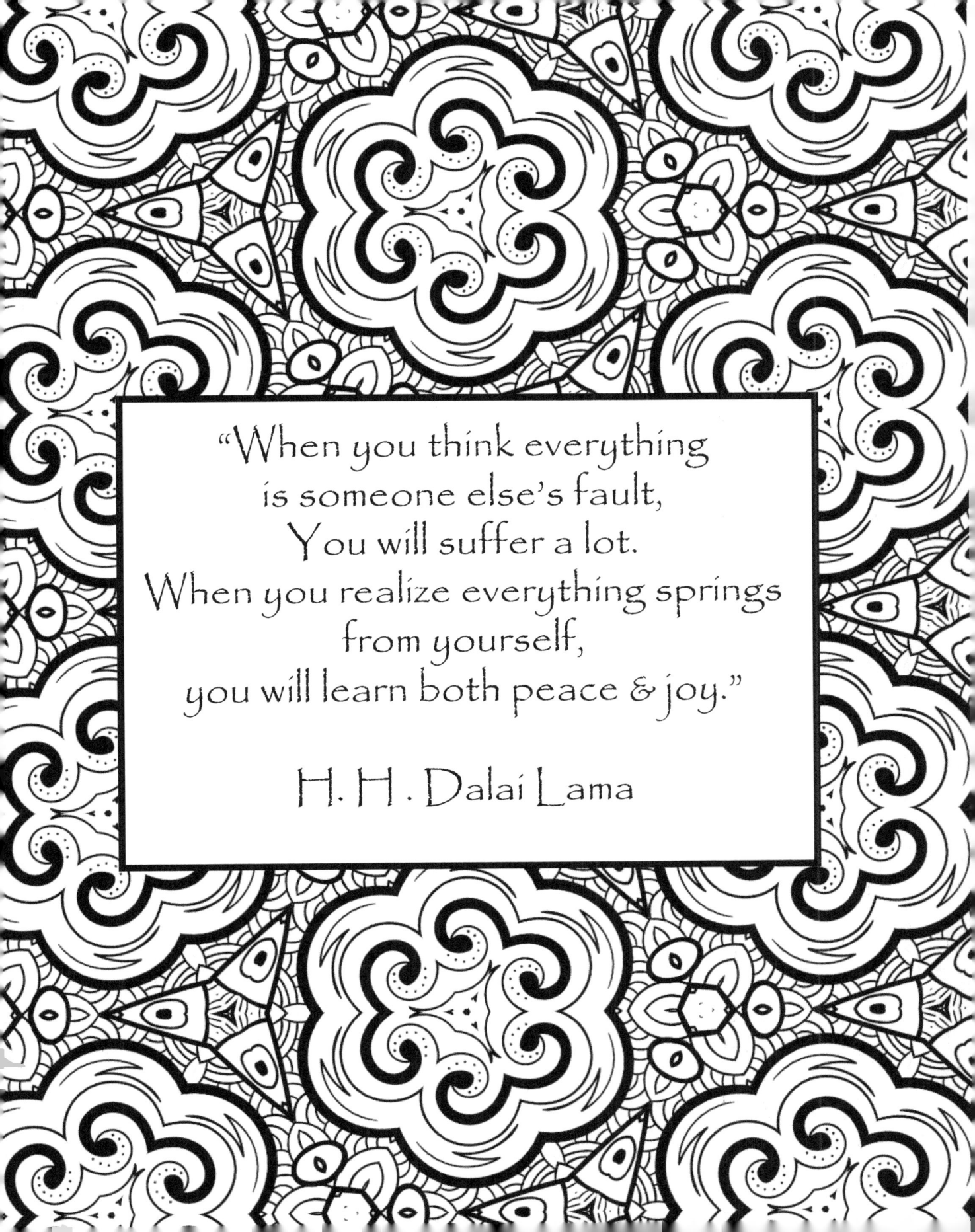

"When you think everything
is someone else's fault,
You will suffer a lot.
When you realize everything springs
from yourself,
you will learn both peace & joy."

H. H. Dalai Lama

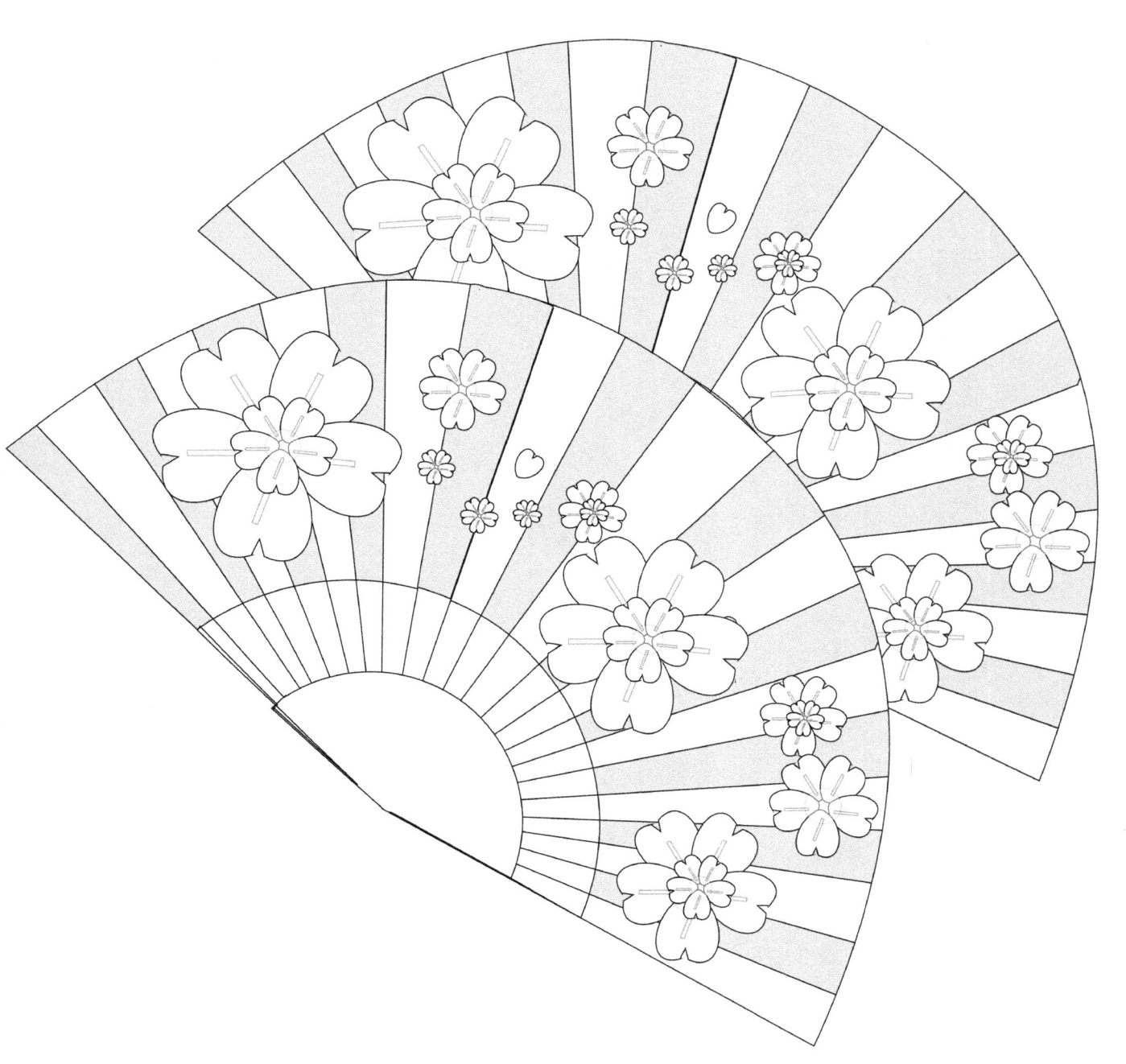

> "I want you to be everything that's you, deep at the center of your being."
>
> — CONFUCIUS

Bonus Designs from Mandalas Volume 2: The Pacific

About Ayesha Hilton

Ayesha Hilton is a creative soul who loves designing coloring pages. She understands the passion and obsession that you may feel when you are coloring. She knows the peace and joy that the simple act of coloring can bring.

Ayesha is also an Amazon bestselling author. Ayesha co-wrote Who Gets the Farm: a practical guide to farm succession planning with her farmer husband Nick Shady. She has also contributed as a co-author in numerous compilation books.

A woman of many passions, Ayesha utilises her business strategy skills along with her love of book publishing to help entrepreneurs, coaches and business owners grow their profile and their business by becoming a published author. Ayesha runs live book writing retreats and online training to help people get their books out of their heads and hearts and out into the world.

Professionally, she has worn many hats. Ayesha used to be an aid worker in Thailand where she worked with Thai sex workers and then Burmese refugees. She's also worked as an IT consultant and web designer for many years.

She is an advocate for Survivors of Suicide as she has seen too many lives destroyed by suicide. Ayesha is also passionate about helping those less fortunate and proudly supports her friend Dean's Landy's foundation, One Heart, to give love, housing and education to orphaned or abandoned children in Africa.

Ayesha lives in Australia, near her home town of Melbourne, with her husband, their son Spencer, Ayesha's daughter Grace, Ayesha's Dad, affectionately known as Grandpa as well as their Jack Russell Holly.

You can find out more about Ayesha at:

www.AyeshaHilton.com

You can follow her on Facebook at:
www.facebook.com/ayeshahiltonpage

Your Invitation to Join The Inspired Life Club

Love the coloring pages in this book?

Stay up to date with new releases and to get free coloring pages in your inbox, please join our mailing list.

When you join, you will also be invited to join our private Facebook group where you can share your works in progress as well as your finished pieces.

Join Our Mailing List Today

www.MyInspiredLife.Club

myinspiredlife COLORING

Other Books You May Like

If you have enjoyed this book, please check out the other books from My Inspired Life.

New titles are released regularly. Stay up to date with new releases and to get free coloring pages in your inbox, please join our mailing list at:

www.MyInspiredLife.Club

If you love this book, you may enjoy these:

- Artistic Affirmations
- The Four Seasons
- Astro Coloring
- Festivities
- For the Best Mum, Wife, Grandma, Daughter, or Friend

www.ingramcontent.com/pod-product-compliance
Lightning Source LLC
Chambersburg PA
CBHW060456300426
44113CB00016B/2611